CW00796565

Playing Cards: Predicting Your Future
Hali Morag

This easy-to-understand guide will take you step by step through the process of predicting your future. You'll learn how each card has its own special meaning. You'll see how the location of the cards and how they are spread before the reader provide a total, descriptive picture of life and love. Known for their accuracy, the cards will answer your questions about what is awaiting you down the path of life - and how you have the power to redirect your future. The book contains helpful illustrations and instructions, and is an essential part of the new age library.

Hali Morag was born to a family whose origin were in Hungary, a country where Gypsies excelled in the reading of cards. A specialist in Tarot, which he learned from his mother, the author went on to study the art of foretelling the future in playing cards. Morag has a long list of private clients and is the author of guides to Tarot and palmistry. He lives between Israel, India, and France.

ASTROLOG COMPLETE GUIDES SERIES

The Complete Guide to Coffee Grounds and Tea Leaf Reading
Sara Zed

The Complete Guide to Palmistry
Batia Shorek

The Complete Guide to Tarot Reading
Hali Morag

Crystals - Types, Use and Meaning
Connie Islin

The Dictionary of Dreams
Eili Goldberg

Meditation: The Journey to Your Inner World
Eidan Or

Playing Cards: Predicting Your Future
Hali Morag

Day-by-Day Numerology
Lia Robin

Using Astrology To Choose Your Partner
Amanda Starr

PLAYING CARDS

Predicting Your Future

Hali Morag

Astrolog Publishing House

Astrolog Publishing House
P.O. Box 1123, Hod Hasharon 45111, Israel
Tel./Fax: 972-9-7412044
E-Mail: info@astrolog.co.il
Astrolog Web Site: www.astrolog.co.il

© Hali Morag 1998

ISBN 965-494-040-X

All rights reserved. No part of this publication may be reproduced,
stored in a retrieval system, or transmitted in any form or by any
means, electronic, mechanical, photocopying, recording or otherwise,
without the prior permission of the publisher.

Published by Astrolog Publishing House 1998

Distribution:
U.S.A. & CANADA by APG - Associated Publishers Group
U.K. & EUROPE by DEEP BOOKS
EAST ASIA by CKK Ltd.

Printed in Israel
10 9 8 7 6 5 4 3 2 1

Table of Contents

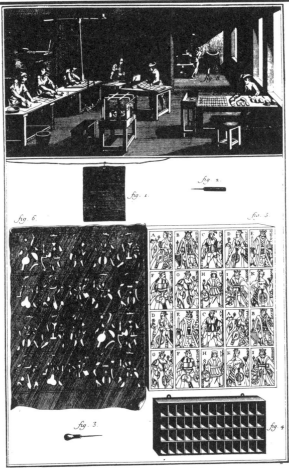

Playing cards were first introduced in Europe in the 15th century. We know of their popularity largely due to the fact that in different locations, it was forbidden by decree to play cards during the week. This was meant to prevent people from playing cards while at work. In the beginning, cards were drawn by hand, using stencils, as shown in the illustration. With the development of the printing press, cards became cheaper and available to everyone.

Introduction

When we speak of predicting the future with regular playing cards, the customary interpretive modes familiar to those who read Tarot cards must be slightly altered. In general, playing cards are much more "closed" - in other words, each card has its own special meaning, and the relative location of a card in the overall interpretation is determined by the order of the cards in the entire spread laid out in front of the reader.

To a certain extent, playing cards resemble the Minor (Lesser) Arcana of the Tarot - four suits of "numerological" cards, ranging from 1 to 10, totaling 40 cards. (The Ace is card number 1 in each suit.) In addition, there are a dozen "royal" cards in each suit - Jack, Queen and King. In other words, there is a grand total of 52 cards. Some readers call the twelve royal cards the "family cards." A few also use the Joker - and then its role is similar to that of the Fool Card in the Tarot. When it appears in a spread, the cards are reshuffled and spread again. Alternatively, the spread is divided into two separate spreads, with the Joker in between, and each is interpreted separately.

As opposed to the Tarot, which has not only the numerological number and symbol, but also a picture - allowing the reader a broad scope of interpretation - playing cards give us closed and exact definitions. The only thing that is possible, and desirable, to combine with the analysis of playing cards is the numerological interpretation of the 40 numbered cards, as well as the "family" interpretation of the "royal" cards.

It is important to remember that each numerical card has a numerological definition. The first and tenth cards - the Ace and the 10 - are both defined as number 1.

As opposed to the Tarot, the single playing card has hardly any meaning at all, and is only significant within the framework of the spread. Therefore, the spreads used here contain many cards. Most readers agree that a minimum of nine cards is needed for reading playing cards.

Playing cards are divided into four suits according to the symbols Diamonds, Clubs, Hearts and Spades. Each of the four suits is connected to one of the four elements - air, water, earth and fire - or to the four seasons. The color of the cards has no importance whatsoever.

Reading Playing Cards

The reading of playing cards is a relatively new art, since these cards became popular only during the last few centuries. It appears that they are a development of the Tarot, and are sometimes known as a "Beggar's Tarot" or the "Tarot's poor relation."

There are strict rules governing the interpretation of playing cards. These rules pertain to the different types of spreads, and to the information which may be gleaned from the cards. Some readers rely solely on the "royal" cards, while others only use cards from number 7 and up. However, most readers prefer to use the full deck of 52.

In this book, we will present the most comprehensive interpretation of the 52 cards. We will start by reminding the reader that any method requiring a spread of seven cards or more - nine cards or more being even more desirable - is sufficient. In other words, to read playing cards, we may utilize all the Tarot spreads, even though we will also offer spreads which are unique to playing cards.

The definitions assigned to each card are rigid. To a great extent, their interpretation is predominantly "West

European". (For example, see the connection to hair color.) In addition, we will present in detail the different combinations which, when they appear together in a spread, have a reinforced validity, or specific meaning - such as three Queens, a Straight, etc.

We will present the suits, followed by the spreads and ending with the special interpretations.

Diamonds

The suit of Diamonds relates mainly to material life - occupation, job, career, professional know-how, promotions, the home (and not necessarily the family, but the actual residence), economic changes, physical activities such as sports or hobbies involving the body, vacations, trips, travel and the fulfillment of one's dreams in the material realm. It is important to note that this suit corresponds to Spring - in other words, the season of beginnings.

[In every interpretation remember the numerological number, from 1 to 9 (10 is actually the number 1 at a higher level), and add the numerological interpretation to complete the picture.]

The interpretations discussed here do not take into consideration the position of the card - reverse or direct ; they deal with cards in this or that spread. If one wants to extend the interpretation to include the card's position, direct or reverse, positive or negative - this may be done. We feel that the order of the cards in a spread, and not their position, is the key to interpretation.

1 (or Ace) of Diamonds

This signifies a beginning, the start of spring, a new job, a new home. Beginnings always bring with them hope for a positive change in direction, usually accompanied by movement upward on the ladder of success.

2 of Diamonds

This indicates money. A card which speaks of an action which will mainly lead to financial reward. However, since it also contains a degree of partnership, it may point to a strong connection with a spouse or business partner. In any case, it may be interpreted as referring to cooperation with another. Stability. Reliability. Only on rare occasions, when the environment of the card is bad, does it hint at contradictions such as a man whose lover is more important to him than his wife, or a person who is involved in two conflicting business partnerships. Some claim that this is a card of "delay," since it shows that the querent [the person whose cards are being read] will have to seek a second opinion before acting.

3 of Diamonds

To a certain extent, this card serves as a bridge between the realms of the spiritual and the material, but with a strong tendency towards the material realm. In other words, it conveys something about professional instruction, goal-oriented education, and training directed toward any practical objective. At the same time, this card may indicate strife - clashes between members of a couple or business partners, and conflicts and problems in the material world resulting from bureaucracy or courtcases.

4 of Diamonds

This is a slow card which steadies, delays and slows down the regular things in life. It is a "basic" card, in the sense that it hoards the labors of the querent bit by bit. But it is also delaying, since it does not allow one to shorten the path to one's achievements by skipping required steps. When this card is in a good spread, it may indicate an upcoming inheritance or the attainment of a long-awaited goal. In a spread, in most cases, this card gives the instruction, as it were, that "what can be put off until tomorrow, may as well be put off until the day after tomorrow." Hence, the card does not contribute to the querent's development.

5 of Diamonds

This is a multi-faceted card; somewhat surprising. It may predict unexpected winnings, a sudden inheritance, surprising positive or negative tidings, pregnancy or interruption of pregnancy, bad news, particularly relating to money matters, significant but involuntary changes, or dangerous diseases. In other words, this card may be interpreted in accordance with its surrounding. It is associated mainly with sudden news which might be good or bad, depending on the context.

6 of Diamonds

This card is sometimes referred to as the "Concluder". It brings to a close the querent's interactions and issues in the economic realm: a marriage of convenience, the purchase of a home, signing a contract, investing...and all that is related to bureaucracy and legal contracts. The establishment is good to him. Formal, institutionalized aspects are included in the spread containing this card. Note: In a bad order of cards, this card may also be interpreted as a breaking or repudiation of all legal frameworks. In other words, it may have a negative meaning.

7 of Diamonds

This cards offers power, vigor and momentum to any material process in which the querent is involved. To some extent, it is a card that helps a person "shift gears" and shoot forward. It also indicates that *now* is the time for him to make a move; otherwise, he will miss the opportunities presently opening up to him. When one does not act with the required speed and energy, the card predicts a quick fall.

The 7 of Diamonds presents new possibilities, not to be missed. For this reason, this card is known as "The Open Door" in Italy.

8 of Diamonds

This card resembles card 4 in that it is a delaying or slowing card. However, the 8 brings the entire system to a complete halt - such as in the case of a religious holiday, a general strike or a vacation. The querent's situation, relative to his starting point, does not deteriorate. Furthermore, the card frequently teaches that *now* is the time to take a break and stop a process, by "retiring" for a short or long period of time. In the area of health, this card indicates a long period of treatment - perhaps surgery or hospitalization. In any case, this card freezes the existing conditions and stops everything the person is doing.

9 of Diamonds

This is a good card, which presents a person with many possibilities. It hints at possible promotion, economic prosperity, a successfully met challenge, a good business trip, or a change for the better which occurred or will do so in the future. It is a dynamic card which has the ability to change the querent's life quickly from one extreme to another.

10 of Diamonds

This card repeats the message of card number 1 but much more strongly. Actually, the card teaches the querent that it is time for him to increase the scale of what he has accomplished until now - from small to big! It is an important card, particularly at the end of a spread.

Jack of Diamonds

Like other royal cards, this card defines people's character traits.The role of these traits in the life of the person whose cards are being read, or of the reader, is revealed by the order of the cards in the spread. It indicates a young, successful person with a smooth path and bright future ahead of him or her. There is no doubt that the card points to an individual who will acquire a high-status profession and achieve true recognition. In addition, this young person is amiable and popular.

Queen of Diamonds

This card indicates a man or woman who is light-haired and authoritative, and has gone far in his/her career. At the same time, it is an indication of complete authority at home. When a woman gets this card, it generally shows it is she who wears the pants around the house. It also attests to a practical and stable nature, a good reputation, patience, and good health.

King of Diamonds

Highest authority. This card usually indicates a mature man with formal authority (such as a judge, rabbi, priest, etc.) or a grandfather who exerts a strong influence over the person. The card does not always present a pleasant picture; however, it always attests to an overriding authority. The card is particularly important when it appears in the center of a spread, and mainly when the cards are being read for a man who has reached maturity but is not yet middle-aged.

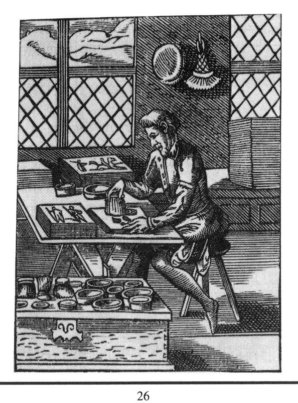

Clubs

People who predict the future with playing cards tend to jest, "Clubs are more lucrative than dollars!" This is quite true. Indeed, the suit of Clubs mainly deals with money issues: income, financial risks, inheritance, debts, investments, distribution of wealth, lotteries, etc. In short, it fuels the entire system!

This is the importance of the suit. Clearly, in each spread there is an attempt to focus its theme - to know, for example, the origin of the inheritance, or, in another instance, where danger might lurk. In order to focus on a particular subject, the suit of Clubs is aided by other cards.

Incidentally, clubs are linked to the summer. And like the summer, their interpretations are for the most part dry and to the point.

1 (or Ace) of Clubs

This is an unstable card, indicating money that appears quickly... and disappears just as quickly. This card is useful mainly for people who deal in economic enterprises, and who are likely to suddenly win or lose large sums of money: an unexpected inheritance; winning a lottery. In a figurative sense, it might indicate marriage, pregnancy or birth.

2 of Clubs

An economic opponent is undermining attempts at rapid advancement. This card attests to an obstacle which the querent must overcome, but does not say what that obstacle might be. After this stumbling block has been removed - usually without any relation to the querent's actions - true success can be expected.

3 of Clubs

This card resembles the Wheel of Fortune Card in the Tarot. It opens up one's luck once again and offers another chance to someone who has experienced economic failure. One might say that it is a gift of fate. But it is important to note its location in the spread. In a "bad" environment, this card predicts that one is on the verge of a fall!

4 of Clubs

This card warns of danger from scoundrels, scam artists, thieves, and the like. This danger is derived from the environment in which the querent is active. It is important to understand that this card, whose number actually indicates stability (in the numerological context), presents the querent's economic activities as a challenge to the environment which is attempting to exploit him.

5 of Clubs

This card carries with it the querent's economic situation, from the past until the present day - a legacy and gifts which he received, various documents testifying to the ownership of property, family connections, family status, etc. It also includes everything related to contracts and lawyers, courtcases or bureaucratic procedures. This card derives its precise interpretation from the spread in which it appears. Positioned at the end of a spread, the card may indicate that the querent's heirs will soon bequeath his property!

6 of Clubs

This card opens up new opportunities ranging from new enterprises, a new jobs and travel, to a one-time opportunity for a good investment (particularly in the field of real estate). It should be remembered that this card indicates mobility and its meaning may be altered by different spreads. Interpret it with caution!

7 of Clubs

This card opens up a new direction - but only within the framework of the person's present life and activities. The card hints at promotion, additional responsibilities, or success in a current business venture. However, it does not represent a substantial change, but rather a change already inherent in the development of the overall system. It has a positive connotation, particularly when it appears at the end of a spread or exactly in the center of a spread.

8 of Clubs

Danger! This card - despite its numerological meaning - indicates a passion for gambling in any area related to money. Although the card acquires its precise interpretation from the context in which it appears, the meaning of this card will generally range from negative to extremely negative. A special warning is directed to a woman who wants to get married, especially when this card appears in her prospective husband's spread.

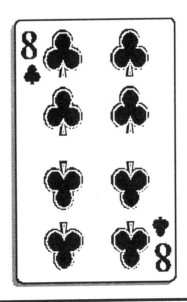

9 of Clubs

A great card! Indicates that the querent is at one with himself regarding his economic activities, which take on a sort of "spiritual" quality - exemplified by the successful entrepreneur or professional whose economic activities bring satisfaction on a spiritual plane. When this card appears in a bad spread, it means that the querent must take himself in hand and continue moving forward, as his own skills will extricate him from any problematic situation. The 9 of Clubs is significant in a woman's spread, particularly when her skills are not reflected from the economic point of view.

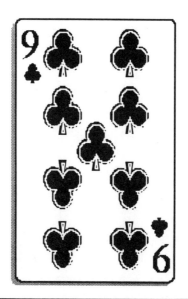

10 of Clubs

This card repeats the message of card number 1 and testifies to good fortune leading to economic security - by way of a legacy, a wedding, a lottery or a successful investment. The exact meaning of this card is derived from the adjacent cards. When a couple have spreads done in parallel, and this card appears in both, it promises success!

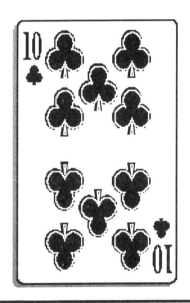

Jack of Clubs

This card testifies to youth, unusual power and energy, a restless character, and a high level of initiative. The excess of energy contained in this card may hint at the nature of the querent, or at the nature of those around him. Pay attention to the entire spread. For example, this card may indicate a mistress who is financially draining her married lover... or an energetic partner who is pushing the cart forwards. Difficult to interpret.

Queen of Clubs

This signifies a very feminine, strong, dark-haired woman, who radiates a positive sexuality and has many ambitions and skills which contribute to success in business. This card connects the series of "Queen" cards to the financial aspect of human relations. Usually, the appearance of this card attests to a good and stable relationship between husband and wife.

King of Clubs

This card indicates a generous person, usually a mature, black-haired, quite good-looking, self-assured, popular individual, who has a respectable reputation. In a spread that refers to a couple's relationship, this card indicates a healthy sexuality. The card's meaning for each individual is determined by its location in the spread. If the card is in the center of a spread, it means that a man is at the center of his extended family.

Hearts

The suit of Hearts is, to a great extent, the most interesting of all the playing card suits. As you may have already guessed, this suit deals with matters of the heart, emotions. This is where we find love and jealousy, marriage and divorce and all matters of romance. It also pertains to family matters and relationships with close friends. Clearly, both betrayals and problems associated with sexual and emotional life are also found here.

In addition to these areas, the Hearts inform us about many other aspects of life. A Hearts card may, for example, indicate if a person is pursuing a certain issue wholeheartedly - an issue brought up in an adjacent card in the spread. Does the person like or dislike the path which has been delineated for him? Does he involve others in his joy and sorrow? There are other examples connected to the overall spread.

The suit of Hearts is compared to the autumn, as it involves rain and wind following a dry spell, emotions in a transitional season. However, when finding a Hearts card in a spread, it is important to interpret the location of the cards cautiously. Take note of the following chapters which speak of special combinations of cards in a spread. In the Hearts suit, the emphasis on combinations such as three Hearts in a row or a pair of royal cards is much more important and decisive than in the other suits.

1 (or Ace) of Hearts

This is a good card. It presents, first and foremost, the family unit of the querent. The precise interpretation will emerge from the adjacent cards in the spread. In any case, this card teaches us the importance of the home, the family, and love in its "institutionalized" forms. The neighboring cards in a spread are interpreted as hints for the meaning of the Ace of Hearts, and not as cards in their own right. In principle, this card generally indicates a positive direction (and the neighboring cards point to the area, time-period or place). This card is particularly important and significant to an individual who is in an emotional crisis; it is a ray of light in the person's life, a ray that penetrates the darkness and brings a positive change to his life.

2 of Hearts

This is a good card which points out that it takes two to tango, as defined by the Italian Method of reading playing cards. It refers to couples' relationships and indicates a new love, a wedding, a romantic meeting or even a good business partnership. In a time of crisis, this card attests to the fact that the wounds of the crisis will heal as if they had never been. Furthermore, when this card appears in a bad spread, predicting bad times, it will mean that it would be possible to overcome these difficulties if only the querent were to find a loving and faithful partner.

3 of Hearts

This card indicates that the querent does not know how to channel his feelings. Sometimes it refers to a person with an excess of emotional energy, or the ability to fall in love with anyone (a romantic triangle). It indicates people who fall head over heels in love, and are at a loss. In a good spread, this is a great card, since it indicates the blossoming of love - a first love or a renewed love. In a bad spread, it indicates emotional or sexual problems. Incidentally, this card also points out problems and their solutions in the area of sexuality.

4 of Hearts

This is a card that brings everything to a halt. Although it is a Hearts card, it is interpreted as the card of stagnation. To a great extent, the querent loses his ability to love and to forge an emotional connection. (The reasons for this phenomenon become clear when the adjacent cards are examined.) The problem is that no solution can be seen in the immediate future. Actually, the only solution is to begin a new relationship, or to revitalize the previous, stagnant connection fundamentally. One might say that the 4 of Hearts (particularly if next to another Hearts card) indicates a later period in life, one in which the querent has already experienced a "great love", has been burnt and has survived.

It is an excellent card if it appears prior to a second marriage. Problematic in the case of sexual difficulties. A card which raises questions whenever it appears in the spread of a young man or woman!

5 of Hearts

This card is like an alarm, a red light at an emotional crossroads. This is the time to pull yourself together, hide emotional troubles and move forward. The querent alone can extricate himself from the morass of jealousy, stagnation and depression to which this card attests. Now is the time to review the past - erase it - and look hopefully towards the future! The card indicates that the querent has a great number of emotional problems. However, it also points out that the opportunity exists for him to solve his problems. In a good spread, the adjacent cards will show the querent which direction he must take. It is a dangerous card when surrounded by Diamonds.

In an odd-numbered spread, when this card is exactly in the middle, it may indicate jealousy which is liable to lead to extreme violence.

6 of Hearts

This card is mainly a "general" card; it indicates the degree to which the querent is integrated into broader frameworks in society, his extended family and circle of friends. It is also the card that indicates a person who can be described as "good" or "kind" in the same way that a girl can be described as a "good girl". While this is not serious praise, the direction is positive. It is most important to understand that the center of this card is "compromise" - a person who will do anything to compromise rather than quarrel or come into conflict. In a bad spread, the card is likely to indicate an emotionally dependent person. In a good spread, it testifies to a person who sticks to the middle path, without ups or downs.

It is an important card for a woman who wants to know about the men who are interested in her.

7 of Hearts

This card may be described as the card of the emotions in dreams. It attests to a person's ambitions, dreams, fantasies, heroes, etc. One might add that this card is the most romantic in the whole deck. It turns every real issue into a dream come true! However, this card may have its disadvantages too. At times, the card indicates a tendency to ignore reality and sink into romantic fantasies. Thus, the individual will display real mystical romanticism, or have a tendency to be "love-sick". It is particularly dangerous for women who have suffered a broken heart in the past.

8 of Hearts

This card is a warning. The querent is so heavily entrenched in his emotions that he does not see what is happening before his eyes! This card also indicates that he knows no bounds and does not differentiate between what he desires and what is actually available to him, or between what is revealed and what is concealed. As a rule, it is a positive card (since it warns against danger) and in a good spread it becomes more positive. In a bad spread, the card is still basically positive. However, the warning "Don't go too far!" is far more important.

9 of Hearts

This card sums up the querent's ambitions or heart's desire in his present stage of life. By looking at the neighboring cards we can determine his ambitions - love, money, success, a good reputation and honor - or negative emotions, such as lust for revenge, self-destruction, etc. The degree to which these desires will be fulfilled is determined by the cards that follow this one in the spread. If it is the final card in the spread, it indicates a negative direction.

10 of Hearts

This is a good card which testifies to happiness and wealth, love and friendship, romance and good feelings... In other words, it is similar to the Ace in the suit. However, as opposed to the first card, the 10 of Hearts appears after crises or difficult situations, and indicates that the querent will overcome the troubles he experienced in the past. The cards preceding this card in a spread indicate the source of the problems, while the cards following this card will suggest how to surmount them. This is an important card in any spread.

Jack of Hearts

This card speaks of a person who is admired by a younger acquaintance, and must be interpreted accordingly. If the querent is a man, it might refer to a young, innocent female partner; if it is a woman, it might refer to a young son, etc. By examining the adjacent cards, we may attempt to understand the direction or the subject to which the card alludes. When we have identified the figure, this card acts as "Eros" - sending arrows of love into the heart of the beloved.

Queen of Hearts

This card signifies motherhood, stability, the home and the security of having emotional support which one seeks, and receives, from one's mother. It is important to grasp that this card represents the ideal of motherhood. It appears, for example, in a man's spread, especially if he is searching for a woman with his mother's character. The card is important on its own, but it is also important to note that its significance derives not just from the neighboring cards, nor from itself. It does have significance on its own with regard to problems of infertility or pregnancy.

King of Hearts

This card represents established, stable emotions, and romance "as it appears in books". The entire spread is overshadowed by the love of a respectable, solid man (or woman) who acts in accordance with social norms and with the demands of his or her status. It is a difficult card to interpret. Some readers make their work easy by interpreting it as concerning a relationship with a widow or widower (or someone who is divorced). But this is not always the case. It is important to consider the other royal cards in the spread and judge this card within the context of the overall combination of all the royal cards, without reference to their suit.

Spades

The suit of Spades is, to some extent, a negative suit. It speaks of trouble, problems and mishaps. However, on the other hand, that is precisely the goal of predicting the future with cards...to warn against trouble, problems and mishaps!

In other words, the Spades Suit is the warning signal of the deck and issues these warnings, regarding divorce, illness, separation, etc., in a direct manner. It says, "Be Careful!" or "Danger Ahead!" regarding the entire spread, or adjacent cards in the spread.

Spades correspond to the cold and bleak winter. And before discussing these "cold" cards, it is worth noting once again that that is their precise objective: to warn against possible trouble and problems! In this way, the querent knows what is awaiting in the future and can plan his steps and actions in a manner which will allow him to prevent, confront or soften the blows coming his way.

Remember to take this into account when analyzing the Spades cards in a spread. In addition, don't forget to include the numerological interpretation of each card - which will usually prove to be rather bleak!

1 (or Ace) of Spades

This indicates the end - a bad end. Death. Permanent separation. It is a bad card, which signifies the end of a process, an irreversible ending. Many readers call this card the "payment" card: the querent is paying for the many bad deeds he committed during the course of his lifetime. In order to identify the source of an ominous fate or the reason why he is paying for his actions, the adjacent cards must be examined. Only with their aid can the situation be interpreted.

This is a very bad card when it appears at the end of a spread. When it appears at the beginning of a spread, some readers collect the cards, reshuffle the deck and spread the cards again. This latter spread is *never* changed.

When the querent is interested in learning about his spiritual make-up, this card serves as the card of "fate" - it draws a person's karma from one generation to another.

2 of Spades

This card speaks of separation or distancing, and warns of a break in an important life process. Usually this refers to a separation of a married couple, divorce, betrayal, etc. However, this card may also allude to corruption, embezzlement or bribery. In any case, regarding the querent, this card warns of an ominous situation. When inquiring about a business partner, and this card appears - beware! When a husband asks about his wife, or a wife about her husband, it indicates infidelity which will end in an irreversible separation. When examining matters of health, this card alludes to a serious operation or the removal of an organ. A difficult card.

3 of Spades

In Italy this card is known as "The Love Triangle". It signifies that a third party has intervened in the couple's relationship, particularly in the area of sex, and is disrupting their lives. It is important to remember that this is not always a matter of a lover. A family member - even a child - may be the cause of the disruption. Remember too that this card indicates that "someone close to you" will come between you and your beloved. The spread may hint at who it might be. Incidentally, in a good spread, the card may allude to a new romantic connection or a journey.

4 of Spades

Life isn't fair! This card indicates that the querent is stuck, to all intents and purposes. He feels at a low point in life and cannot extricate himself: financial difficulties, conflict, problems with government administration, bureaucracy and the law. It is difficult to find understanding and assistance. The spread can enlighten us as to the cause of the situation, but not as to how to remedy it.

5 of Spades

Brakes. Inhibitions. This card blocks a person, particularly in the spiritual realm, preventing success. This card speaks of illness, listlessness, "behavioral anemia". In a bad spread, it indicates a malignant disease! If this card appears in a spread, it is important for the querent to identify the source of his depression and try to distance himself from it. If the inquiry concerns a third person, this card indicates that that person has a negative personality.

6 of Spades

Tomorrow will be a better day! This card brings a weak ray of light to the gloomy Spades. Although it means that the querent is caught in an unpleasant situation (this can be seen in the surrounding cards), this card predicts that the situation will eventually change, and allows him to hope. We must take note that this card is a "pusher"; when it is in a spread, it pushes good cards out. For example, if it appears in the spread of a single woman, she will not marry until she has eradicated the factor that is causing her harm at present (and then the card will disappear from the spread). The problem lies in whether this factor is actually her very state of being single - and she cannot marry until she eradicates it!

In this case, the card prevails and takes control of the person's life.

7 of Spades

This card is like a stumbling block in the path of a blind man. However, it is the querent himself who is the blind man. In other words, he is causing himself to stumble because of one of his character traits. One might say that his problems are his own fault. This card stands alone with no connection to neighboring cards. It warns the querent about himself alone.

8 of Spades

This is a difficult card, which hints of future social problems and trouble from the establishment or the legal system. The spread does not always reveal the exact cause, but the card warns of difficult problems. It also attests to a closed person, a "loner", even if the other cards in the spread do not point in that direction.

9 of Spades

This card, as is evident from its well-known numerological interpretation, is the finishing point. The combination of the numerological meaning with Spades deals the hardest blow of all. The person is now at his lowest ebb, down and out, and does not know if he will ever be able to rise again.

10 of Spades

This card repeats the message of the Ace, but indicates that the querent is embroiled in a series of troubles (which may be discerned from the adjacent cards in the spread). A difficult card.

Jack of Spades

The Jack of Spades speaks of someone who is not close to the querent, a young, noble-minded individual, but with whom any connection means trouble! Even when the spread speaks of romance or successful business ventures, it warns that it will come to a bad end. If the card is interpreted as pertaining to the querent, it tells of someone who moves around in social circles but who cannot find a place for himself anywhere.

Queen of Spades

This is a difficult card. A widow, a hardened single woman - lonely and emotionally handicapped. Totally blocked! (Therefore, the remaining cards in the spread have no effect on her.) Be careful when this figure appears in a spread, particularly if it represents the querent. In Italy, it is known as "The House Witch."

King of Spades

This indicates a difficult man, particularly when the card speaks of the querent. This card alludes to a man who is used to a rigid and fastidious lifestyle, and is trying to impose it on everyone around him. It is difficult to live in the vicinity of such a person and even more difficult to be under his authority.

Now that we know the playing cards, we will move on to the "tricks" used in interpreting them, and the various and special spreads for playing cards, including the differentiation between the different methods.

The English Method

Playing cards may be spread according to any spread which is applicable to the Tarot cards. However, there are also special and unique methods for spreading playing cards, and these will be discussed below. In general, the alternative methods are divided into two divisions: the English Method and the Italian Method.

In the English Method, each card has one meaning only. In other words, there is no significance to a direct or reverse card. All 52 cards are used, i.e. there are 13 cards in each of the four suits.

The basis of the English Method is the principle of "conscious choice". The reader scrutinizes the querent (or acquires a detailed description of him), and chooses from the deck a unique card which will serve as the "Significator Card" in each and every type of spread he uses.

The Significator Card

The Significator Card is chosen according to gender, age and hair color of the querent. These factors are always divided into two categories: man/woman, age over 40/ under age 40, light hair/dark hair.

Consequently, there are eight possibilities for the Significator Card (other cards cannot serve as the Significator Card in the English Method):

Man - light-haired - age 40+ corresponds to King of Diamonds
Man - light-haired - age 40- corresponds to King of Hearts
Man - dark-haired - age 40+ corresponds to King of Spades
Man - dark-haired - age 40- corresponds to King of Clubs

Woman - light-haired - age 40+ corresponds to the Queen of Diamonds
Woman - light-haired - age 40- corresponds to the Queen of Hearts

Woman - dark-haired - age 40+ corresponds to the Queen of Spades

Woman - dark-haired - age 40- corresponds to Queen of Clubs

After the reader chooses the appropriate Significator Card, he asks the querent to shuffle the deck; the reader then takes the cards and spreads them face down, in a fan shape.

The 18-Card Spread

The most popular spread in the English Method is the 18-Card Spread.

The Significator Card is placed on the table facing downwards. The querent chooses a card from the fan of cards on the table and places it on the table, face up, at the upper left-hand corner of the Significator Card. The second card he chooses is placed above the Significator Card; the third, in the upper right-hand corner; the fourth, to the left of the Significator Card, and the fifth, to the right of the Significator Card, from left to right. Three additional cards are placed under the Significator Card. Finally, the ninth card is placed on top of the Significator Card, covering it.

Now, the remaining cards in the fan can be shuffled again (they can also be left unshuffled) and eight more cards are chosen. These are placed on the cards surrounding the Significator Card. (No additional card is placed on the Significator Card.) This concludes the spread... and now all that remains is to interpret the cards!

Note that we have nine pairs. Each pair of cards has a meaning pertaining to a certain area of life. The exact interpretation is determined by the two neighboring cards. During the second stage, it is determined by the cards adjacent to the pair. Also, the Significator Card is given a special interpretation in accordance with the actual situation of the querent.

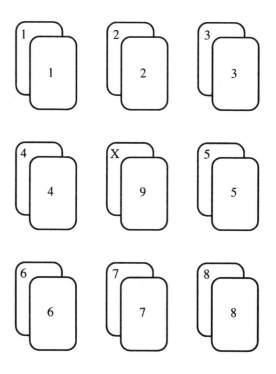

The Significator Card is marked with an X.

Look at the diagram and remember:

The first pair speaks of the querent's past when he was still dependent on his parents.

The second pair tells about the querent's past from the time he reached adulthood and independence up until the present day.

The third pair is indicative of the past year.

The fourth and fifth pairs, on both sides of the Significator Card, speak of difficulties or breakthroughs in the querent's life.

The sixth pair speaks of what is expected in the coming year of the querent's life.

The seventh pair points to the querent's future, for as long as he is independent and self-supporting.

The eighth pair tells about his future, when he will be dependent on others and supported by them.

The pair consisting of the ninth card and the Significator Card is actually the character analysis of the querent.

This spread is useful and easy to interpret. The use of two cards in each category supports the interpretation. Note that after taking in the information from the Significator Card, the interpretation must be done from left to right and from top to bottom: in other words, from the distant past to the distant future.

The Traditional Spread

Another spread, used mainly for reading playing cards with the English Method, is the traditional Gypsy Spread (as opposed to the Gypsy Spread used for Tarot cards).

In this spread, too, the reader first chooses the Significator Card and lays it on the table, face up. Next, the querent shuffles the cards, cuts the deck into two, and hands half a deck to the reader. The rest of the cards are put aside. The reader takes the cards and chooses 21 cards, spreading them in threes, from left to right. Note that in this spread, three consecutive cards are placed one on top of the other, face up. The final spread has 22 cards, similar to the Major Arcana of the Tarot.

Each group of three cards indicates a different area, and all cards are interpreted in accordance with the Significator Card "overseeing" them. The interpretation is done from left to right.

The first threesome teaches about the personality of the querent, his spiritual state and mental state.

The second threesome speaks about his present family status.

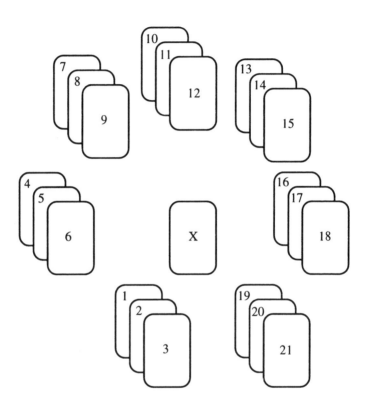

The Significator Card is marked with an X.

The third threesome points to his immediate aspirations.

The fourth threesome indicates his expectations for the future.

The fifth threesome brings destiny or the unexpected into the life of the querent.

The sixth threesome serves to predict the immediate future.

The seventh threesome serves to forecast the distant future.

This spread requires knowledge of the connections between the different cards. This is due to the fact that the circumstances of each threesome are actually determined by the balance of the three different cards, all the while taking into account the Significator Card.

In this spread, the presence of pairs or three of a kind, or of cards with special meanings is of utmost importance, as will be discussed later. Of great consequence is a situation when the Significator Card and the three cards are of the same suit.

The Holy Cross Spread

A third spread used in the English Method is the Holy Cross or Mystics' Spread. Here, too, the reader chooses the appropriate Significator Card and places it in the center of the table. Next, after shuffling the cards, he arbitrarily picks a dozen cards from the deck. He now takes the Significator Card, adds it to the twelve cards, shuffles them all and sets them out one after the other. (See diagram, page 85.)

The first question arising at this point is: Where will the Significator Card turn up? It may appear in the north-south line - the vertical line, and then the interpretation speaks of a person who is being led by destiny, by his environment or by circumstances. However, if the Significator Card appears in the east-west line - the horizontal line, the querent has control over his life and its circumstances. If the Significator Card turns up exactly in the middle, it indicates that the querent's life revolves entirely around himself.

The vertical line is interpreted as the querent's actual, present condition, the fourth card being the center of his life. The horizontal line, cards number 8 to 13 (including card number 4), teaches us about the causes and reasons for his present situation.

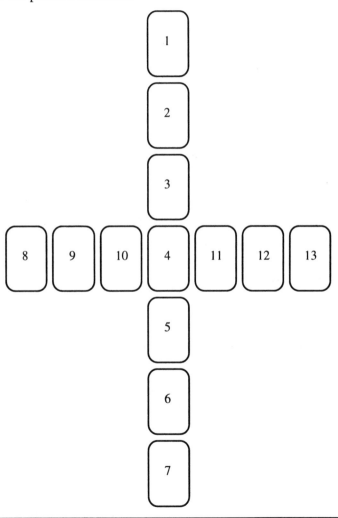

The Italian Method

The Italian Method of reading playing cards is essentially quite different than the English Method. First, in this method only 32 cards are used - the cards from the 7 to the Ace, which is higher than the King, and not card number 1 (although its interpretation is similar).

The second difference, just as significant, is that in the Italian Method each card has a direct and reverse meaning. When the cards are spread, it is immediately evident if a card is direct or reverse. (See below.) If you have a special deck of cards used for predicting the future by this method, mark the bottom of each card in the pack so that you will be able to determine immediately if the card you are choosing is direct or reverse.

Direct or Reverse?

Note that the meaning of direct or reverse is in addition to, or as a completion of, the basic interpretation discussed in the review of the suits.

Diamonds

Ace - Good news. Marriage. A good message.

Reverse - Bad news.

King - A strong man.

Reverse - Scoundrel, traitor.

Queen - A woman with personal charm...and obvious malice.

Reverse - A Gossip.

Jack - A soldier, messenger, an unreliable man.

Reverse - A scoundrel, engenders wickedness.

10 - A change of workplace or residence.

Reverse - A mishap, bad luck.

9 - Inheritance, a win, a gift.

Reverse - A quarrel, family problems.

8 - A vacation, gift or pleasure.

Reverse - A break with a close person, a painful separation.

7 - Good luck, a new opportunity.

Reverse - Severe criticism, harmful gossip.

Clubs

Ace - A marriage of convenience, money, inheritance.

Reverse - Fatigue, the end of happiness.

King - A good person, helpful.

Reverse - A person who is not suited to the position he holds.

Queen - Widow, a hard-hearted woman.

Reverse - Deadly jealousy.

Jack - An admired and beloved young man.

Reverse - An irresponsible young man.

10 - Success, wealth.

Reverse - Economic troubles.

9 - Profit, good opportunities, a good marriage.

Reverse - Minimal profits. Thinking "small."

8 - A great love, happiness.

Reverse - An annoying admirer (male or female). Quarrels.

7 - Mild worries.

Reverse - Major difficulties.

Hearts

Ace - Love, family, happiness.

Reverse - A change, an unexpected development.

King - A handsome, rich, generous man.

Reverse - A fickle, hasty, irresponsible man.

Queen - A beautiful, attractive, loving woman.

Reverse - A disturbing love, a suffering woman.

Jack - A dissolute, single youngman.

Reverse - A young man who is untrustworthy and a liar.

10 - Happiness and wealth.

Reverse - Worry and instability.

9 - Dreams coming true.

Reverse - (temporary) Despair, difficulties.

8 - A good marriage, family, a good trip.

Reverse - Frivolousness.

7 - A balanced life, a person who is satisfied with his life.

Reverse - Health problems. A person who is disappointed with his life.

Spades

Ace - A business or work opportunity.

Reverse - Legal problems, schemes.

King - Widower. Conflicts "within the law."

Reverse - An unscrupulous enemy.

Queen - A single, divorced or widowed woman.

Reverse - A sly woman, a (female) swindler.

Jack - A crude young man.

Reverse - A malicious or unscrupulous man; a traitor.

10 - Bad news. A traffic accident.

Reverse - Death, disease, prison.

9 - Bad luck, an obstacle.

Reverse - Treason. A stab in the back!

8 - Bad news.

Reverse - A family rift. Mourning.

7 - A quarrel, a change in environment.

Reverse - Falling flat on one's face.

These interpretations, which supplement the general interpretations of the suits, only apply to the Italian Method of reading playing cards. However, this method includes other suggestions which are also applicable to the English Method, or any other method of reading cards.

The Dominant Suit

First, we will discuss the phenomenon known as "The Dominant Suit". This occurs when one suit dominates all the others in the spread. It is visible immediately, and it is not necessary to count the cards - what the reader sees at a glance is the determining factor! There will always be only one Dominant Suit.

When a Dominant Suit is present, the overall interpretation is directed as follows:

Diamonds - Life in general, but never in the family framework. The material realm over the spiritual realm.
Clubs - Business, money, social and other contacts.
Hearts - Family, love, sex.
Spades - Bad news!

Pairs, Three of a Kind, Four of a Kind

Situations in which cards of the same number or royal figure appear, such as a pair, three of a kind or four of a kind, are of great importance. Here, too, there is an interpretation of direct or reverse cards (which is not taken into account when applied to the English Method).

It is important to grasp what the interpretation of a pair, three of a kind or four or a kind, as direct or reverse means. In a pair or three of a kind, if one or two cards are reverse, the whole set is considered reverse. In four of a kind, only when three or four cards are reverse, will the set be considered reverse. Pay attention to this, as many readers are not sufficiently aware of this division. And remember - this only applies to the Italian Method. In the English Method, one looks only at the card - not at its direction. In all cases, in a pair, three of a kind or four of a kind, all cards in the set (two, three or four, accordingly) are seen as a uniform group regarding the direct/reverse positions.

Ace

Pair - An imminent marriage.

Reverse - A problematic marriage.

Three of a kind - A love affair.

Reverse - A spouse's betrayal.

Four of a kind - Financial damage, separation from the family and loved ones.

Reverse - Danger looming!

King

Pair - Great success.

Reverse - Caution. Danger expected!

Three of a kind - Successful business.

Reverse - Mishaps and obstacles (may be overcome!)

Four of a kind - Honor and respect. Success at objectives.

Reverse - Troubles.

Queen

Pair - A new acquaintance.

Reverse - Nasty gossip.

Three of a kind - A journey, hospitality.

Reverse - Jealousy, libel.

Four of a kind - Social activity.

Reverse - Scandal, treachery, fraud.

Jack

Pair - A fight, a financial loss.

Reverse - Deep trouble!

Three of a kind - Problems with the family and at home.

Reverse - Trouble with close acquaintances.

Four of a kind - Conflicts.

Reverse - A bitter quarrel.

10

Pair - Good luck. Unexpected success.

Reverse - Lack of funds.

Three of a kind - A financial problem.

Reverse - Financial disaster.

Four of a kind - Luck, ascending the ladder of success.

Reverse - A lengthy period of difficulty.

9

Pair - Monetary profit.

Reverse - Anger endangering one's health.

Three of a kind - Wealth, property, good health.

Reverse - A temporary financial difficulty.

Four of a kind - A happy surprise.

Reverse - Good news will be delayed by about a month.

8

Pair - A love affair.

Reverse - A break in communications
with the environment.

Three of a kind - A good love affair, marriage.

Reverse - Family problems.

Four of a kind - Success following many difficulties.

Reverse - Deep frustration.

7

Pair - A successful love affair is expected.

Reverse - Fraud. An old enemy returns.

Three of a kind - Pregnancy, birth,
a new opportunity.

Reverse - Health problems.

Four of a kind - Troubles.

Reverse - A highly influential enemy is acting against you.

As stated above, when using the English Method, only the direct position is taken into consideration. However, it is given less importance than when applied in the Italian Method. In the Italian Method, the interpretation - direct or reverse - receives full validity.

The Star Spread

The most commonly used spread in the Italian Method is the Star Spread. This is quite a complicated spread which takes a long time to interpret.

First, the reader chooses a Significator Card according to the character of the querent, as described in the English Method and using the same principles. The Significator Card, marked with an X in the diagram, is placed in the center of the table.

Next, the querent takes the remaining 31 cards, shuffles them and gives them to the reader, who then cuts the deck into three equal piles and takes the first card in each pile and places them at the side of the table, face up. These cards are known as "Indicator Cards", and they provide the general prediction regarding the person in question.

The remaining 28 cards are returned to the querent, who shuffles them and hands them to the reader. The latter picks eight cards and places them around the Significator Card, according to the diagram and in the same order. The cards are marked with numbers 1 to 8. In the second round, the reader places an additional card on each card, numbers 9 to 16; and in the final round, he places cards 17 to 24. Altogether, he will use 24 cards to encircle the Significator Card.

Now the interpretation begins. First, the three "Indicator Cards" on the side are interpreted. Next, the star is considered. Each group of three are interpreted on their own, in relation to the Significator Card. After eight interpretations of groups of three are given, the overall interpretation is summarized.

Each group of three has an area of meaning, according to the following order:

A. Future opportunities which are worthwhile for the querent to pursue, with quite a good possibility of success.

B. Obstacles that might prevent taking advantage of the opportunities mentioned in Section A.

C. What is stopping the querent from fulfilling his potential?

D. The burden of the past which the querent carries around with him, particularly a burden that weighs him down.

E. The querent's past, or what he has acquired in his past, including life experience and knowledge.

F. Past accomplishments and their influence on the present and future.

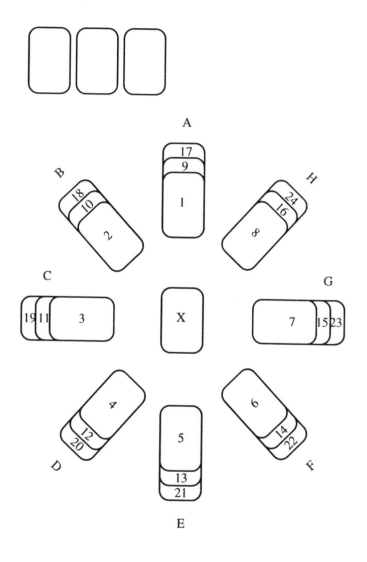

G. What will help the querent to reach his or her goals?

H. Factors that assist the querent to attain his or her goals.

This spread is comprehensive and is also used for reading Tarot cards. It is important to read it according to the order presented here. In particular, when using the Italian Method, pay attention to: the position of the cards, direct or reverse, in each group of three, and in combinations of a pair of cards, three of a kind, or four of a kind (including the Significator Card).

The Fan Spread

This spread is also used in the Italian Method. A bit tricky, it is based in most part on the reader's intuition. It is particularly appropriate for people blessed with a high level of intuition, and who are very experienced in reading cards. At the outset, this spread seems a bit complicated, but after learning and mastering it, it is the easiest and simplest of all.

Thirty-two cards are chosen from the deck. The querent shuffles them, spreads them face down on the table in the shape of a fan, and randomly chooses 13 cards which he hands to the reader. The reader spreads the 13 cards, face up, as an open fan. The reader looks for the Significator Card from among the 13 cards (according to the querent's characteristics). If he has not found the Significator Card, he should choose a 7; if there is more than one 7, he selects the 7 furthest to the left.

If there is neither a Significator Card nor a 7 among the 13 cards, the cards are reshuffled and the procedure is repeated. The procedure may be repeated three times. If after three tries there is no Significator Card or 7, the reading is canceled!

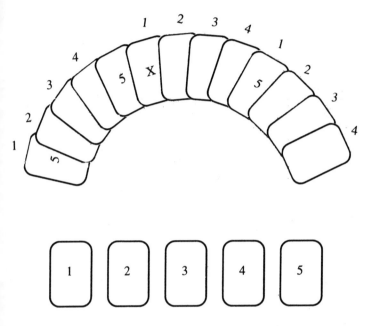

When the Significator Card or the 7 is located - marked by an X in the diagram - this card opens the spread. From this card, we count four cards to the left and pick out the fifth card, to be read. And again, we count four cards and choose the fifth. If necessary, we move from the left end of the fan to the right end, without interrupting the count. In this manner, three cards are chosen, removed from the fan, and spread as the first group of three.

Following the interpretation of the first group of three, the procedure is repeated, and three additional cards are chosen. The count begins, as previously, from the Significator Card, and when one reaches this card again during the fifth round, it is not taken into account. After having interpreted the second group of three, the final group of three is chosen.

At this point, the reader asks the querent to pick five additional cards, and they are spread on the table below the fan. Card number 1 is interpreted with card number 5, card 2 with card 4, and card 3 on its own. In the end, all the separate interpretations are joined together to create one all-encompassing, collective interpretation.

The Week's Spread

When using this spread, the querent shuffles 32 cards and hands them to the reader. In this case, no Significator Card is chosen. The reader spreads the cards in the shape of a fan, and asks the querent to choose randomly 15 cards which are then spread face down in a straight line from left to right, according to the order in which they were selected.

Next, the cards are revealed in pairs, that is, A with A, B with B, etc. The first pair represents tomorrow, the second pair represents the day after tomorrow, and so on, until the end of the coming week. The spread always concerns the day following that on which the spread is being done. Each pair of cards carries the prediction for one of the days of the week, and the central card, alone, predicts the week in its entirety.

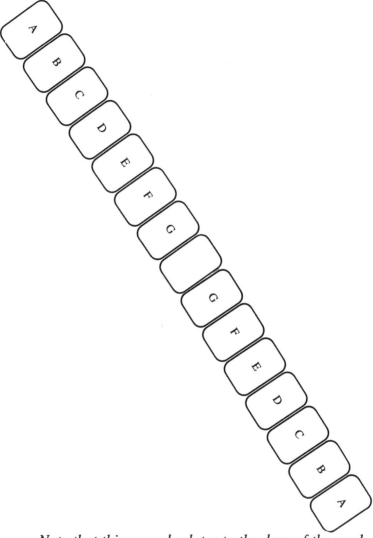

Note that this spread relates to the days of the week and not directly to the querent

Yes, No...Red, Black

This is an amusing spread used for entertainment in the Italian Method. Usually, the individual asks himself a question, the answer to which is "Yes" or "No". He then shuffles the 32 cards, cuts the deck in three, and lays each pile face down on the table.

Next, each pile is turned over - so that the three bottom cards of the piles are visible. At this point, only the *colors* of the cards are considered.

3 red cards - Absolutely yes!

2 red cards - Yes.

3 black cards - Absolutely no!

2 black cards - No.

Indeed, an amusing spread ... and one that generally never misses the mark!

The Central Joker Spread

This spread, known as the Central Joker Spread, or in France as the "Thirteen Lucky Cards", uses the full deck of playing cards. An additional card - the Joker - is chosen and placed in the center of the table, representing the querent. Next, 12 cards are chosen from the pack and placed in consecutive numerical order, as depicted in the diagram.

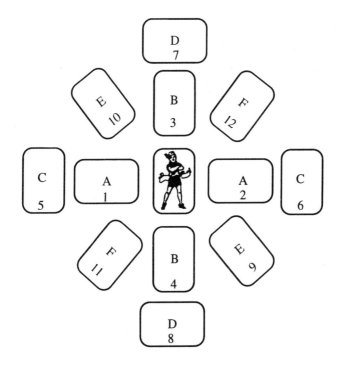

Note the letters which, when coupled, give us six pairs of cards. Each card in a pair is interpreted together with its partner. First cards "A" and "B" are interpreted, which provide us with information concerning the character traits and behavioral patterns of the querent (or alternatively, his present life). Next, cards "C" and "D" are interpreted, predicting his future, in relation to his past. (In other words, a line is drawn from the past to the anticipated future.) Finally, cards "E" and "F" are interpreted, supplementing the information obtained so far by referring to secondary influences which affect the person's life, such as a help or hindrance in his path.

This reading does not take into consideration the position of a card - direct or reverse - but pairs, three of a kind, four of a kind, or Straights, are important.

Various Hints for Correct Interpretation

These short suggestions were accumulated from the experience of card readers. Each reader prepares a list of personal "anchors" which guide his or her reading. When you open the cards, you will accumulate experience which will be expressed in your own "personal anchors."

☞ When using playing cards for reading and predicting the future, a number of cards and combinations of cards, have a special significance in the spread. In other words, they have an importance which goes beyond the cards on their own.

☞ Remember that when discussing the order of the cards, we always refer to the consecutive order in which they are placed on the table, according to the particular spread.

☞ When there is an error in a spread - maybe two cards stuck together or too many cards were chosen from the deck - the cards are reshuffled and re-spread.

☛ The first card in a spread following the choice of the Significator Card has a special significance, as does the last card in a spread.

☛ The playing card deck includes the royal family cards: the King, Queen and Jack. When these three cards appear consecutively - and in this case, their order is not important - the interpretation always concerns the home and the family. When all three are from the same suit, the interpretation is reinforced. In any case, the middle card of the three always indicates the center of the family.

(It is important to remember that this group must include all three cards - Jack, Queen and King. If, for example, there are four consecutive cards - King, Queen, King, Queen - the present interpretation does not apply, since the Jack is missing. And note: The three cards must appear in one single consecutive group.)

☛ When there is a Straight of numerical cards, which appear in ascending or descending order, you can interpret only the last card in the set. A set must include three cards or more.

☛ In every spread, there is a card which is parallel to the card whose meaning is being considered. While using a spread in which the third card from the beginning is examined, the parallel card will be the third card from the end, and so on. If both cards point in the same direction, the meaning derived from the card is reinforced. If the two cards point in different directions, the interpretation is weakened.

☞ The 7 may indicate a great love. Another interpretation of the 7 indicates impotence in a man, or a woman whose passion burns so fiercely that it reaches pathological proportions.

☞ By counting Kings and Queens, it is possible to determine who is the most significant person in the querent's life. First, the Kings and Queens in a spread are counted.

Next, the gender of the querent is added - a King for a man or a Queen for a woman. If the number of Kings is higher than the number of Queens, the most important person in the querent's life is a man, such as a father, husband, etc.

When the number of Queens is higher, the most significant person is a woman.

☞ There is a possibility of using the Joker in the deck being spread. The Joker is used in the same way as the Fool Card in the Tarot. When it turns up in a spread, the cards must be re-spread, or alternatively, the cards may be divided into two different readings, with the Joker separating the two.

Remember that many "anchors" were discussed in the chapters on the Dominant Suit, and in Pairs, Three of a Kind and Four of a Kind.

These hints will help you use playing cards to obtain a precise reading concerning a person's character and past, but mainly to predict his future.